The Violinist's Wedding Album 2
for Violin and Piano

Arranged by Lynne Latham and Catherine McMichael

GRADE 3½

52710444

A Division of **LudwigMasters** Publications
6403 West Rogers Circle • Boca Raton, FL 33487

ABOUT THE ARRANGERS

Lynne Latham (b. 1960) earned a B.M. and M.M. in cello performance from Miami University in Oxford, Ohio. For 20 years, she maintained a private studio of violin, viola, and cello students in the Winston-Salem, North Carolina area. Ms. Latham is a frequent freelance performer and conductor with local chamber groups and orchestras. She is often a clinician/conductor at string clinics and educator conferences throughout the United States. In 1992, Ms. Latham founded Latham Music, a music publishing company specializing in music for strings. In 2007, Latham Music was acquired by The Lorenz Corporation and Lynne was hired as the Executive Editor for Latham Music. She is now the String Editor for LudwigMasters Publications.

Lynne Latham is available as a string clinician. For more information and availability, email lynne@ludwigmasters.com. Presentation topics include full and string orchestra reading sessions, *The Top 10 Things the Band Director Should Know About Teaching Orchestra, Managing Stagefright: Preparing Students for Auditions and Performance, The Thumb Is the Secret (Cello Technique), Fiddling as a Technique Builder, Using Chamber Music in the Classroom, Working With Cello Ensembles, Playing Without Pain, Arranging for Strings, Copyright Jeopardy: What does the law really say?,* and cello or chamber music masterclasses/coaching.

Catherine McMichael, pianist, is a composer, performer, arranger and teacher in Saginaw, Michigan. Her degrees from the University of Michigan are in piano performance and chamber music. Her music is played by professional touring artists, university professors and music students, devoted amateurs and even elementary children on four continents. She is available for commissions for any instrumentation.

Catherine shares her life with her violinist husband, Rod Bieber, and two spirited and musical children, Meredith and Nathan. Rounding out the menagerie are a serene cat and two quizzical dogs. To contact Catherine or hear more of her music, visit www.catherinemcmichael.com.

The Violinist's Wedding Album 2
1. Selections from *The Four Seasons*

Antonio Vivaldi
Arranged by Lynne Latham

12

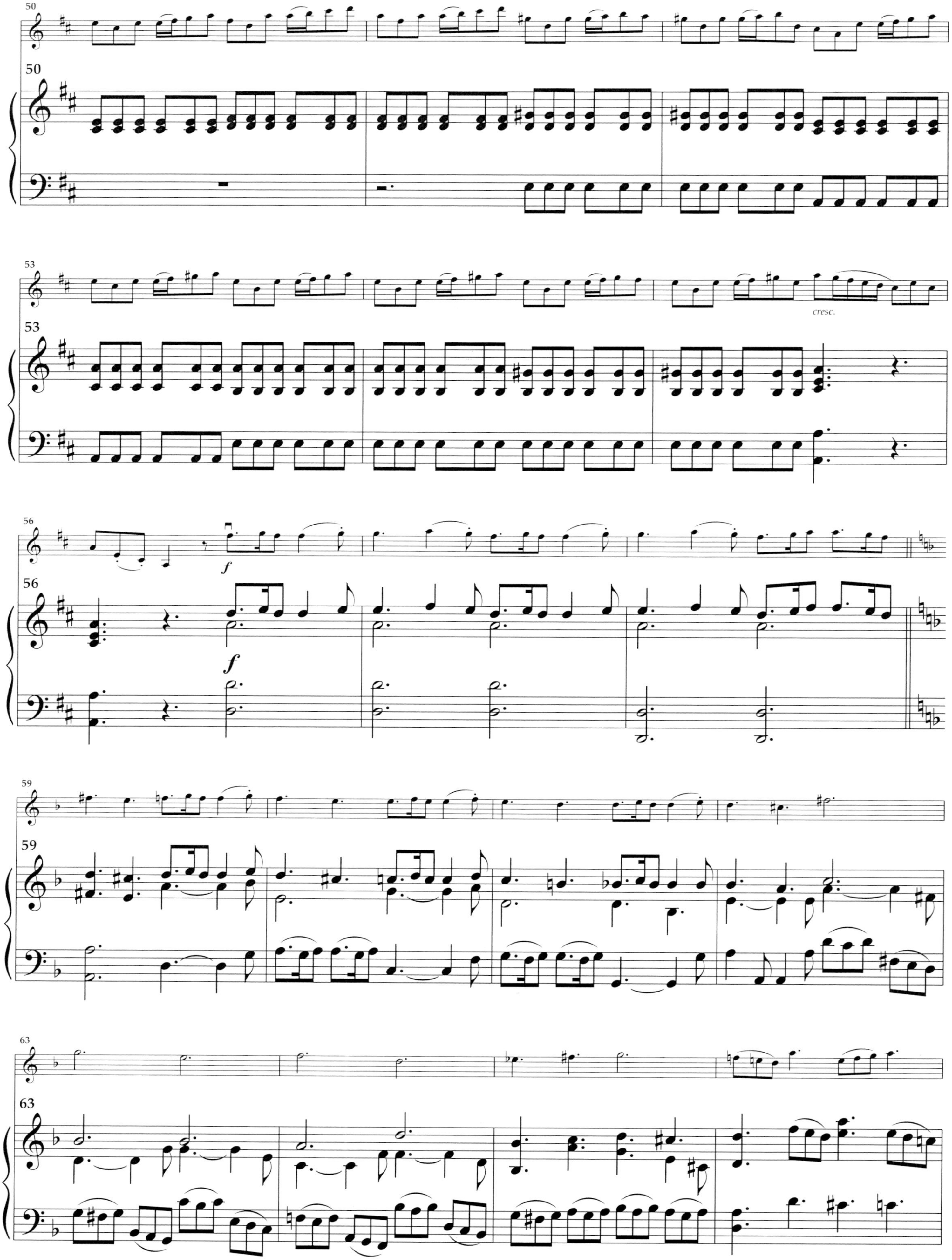

2. Gymnopédie No. 1

Erik Satie
Arranged by Lynne Latham

3. To A Wild Rose

Edward MacDowell
Arranged by Lynne Latham

24

4. Laudate Dominum

Wolfgang Amadeus Mozart
Arranged by Lynne Latham

52710444

5. If With All Your Hearts from *Elijah*

Felix Mendelssohn
Arranged by Lynne Latham

6. Movement 1
from *Brandenburg Concerto No. 3*

Johann Sebastian Bach
Arranged by Lynne Latham

Performance Note: Play 8th notes with a slight separation. 16th notes should be played legato.
No pedal should be used.

52710444

36

7. O Perfect Love

Joseph Barnby
Arranged by Catherine McMichael

8. Adagio from *Sonate Pathétique*

Ludwig van Beethoven
Arranged by Lynne Latham

52710444

52710444

9. Clair de Lune

Claude Debussy
Arranged by Lynne Latham

52710444

52710444

52710444

10. La Fille aux Cheveux de Lin

Claude Debussy
Arranged by Lynne Latham

11. My Heart Ever Faithful

Johann Sebastian Bach
Arranged by Lynne Latham

48

52710444